Message to
a Grandchild

Message to a Grandchild

PETER VANCE

SIDGWICK & JACKSON

First published 2003 by Sidgwick & Jackson
an imprint of Pan Macmillan Ltd
Pan Macmillan, 20 New Wharf Road, London N1 9RR
Basingstoke and Oxford
Associated companies throughout the world
www.panmacmillan.com

ISBN 0 2830 7378 0

1 3 5 7 9 8 6 4 2

Extract from *The Wrong Boy* © W. R. Limited 2000,
published by Black Swan, London, 2001. Reproduced with kind permission of the author.
'Desiderata' © Max Ehrmann 1927, reproduced with kind permission from Robert L. Bell.

A CIP catalogue record for this book is available from
the British Library.

Designed and typeset by Louise Millar
Printed and bound in Great Britain

To Nana

I miss your smile…

Foreword
by Anne Robinson

Towards the end of 2000 Peter Vance wrote to me out of the blue. He told me his nan had Alzheimer's disease and she'd had it for as long as he could remember and Peter relied on other members of his family to tell him what she was like and the kind of things she used to say and do. Having lost my mother to Alzheimer's disease, his letter struck a chord. Alzheimer's can be a cruel visitor to the family. It doesn't announce its arrival and it creeps into your home. The person's loss of memory is keenly felt by those around them for whom such memories and experiences have often been a guiding hand in the past.

Peter's book is a wonderful thing; he put it together himself and wrote to all the contributors. And, of course, he arranged for the Alzheimer's Society to benefit from the book's sales.

There are more than 700,000 people living with Alzheimer's or another form of dementia in the UK. The Alzheimer's Society believes in every case that it's the individual who is the most important.

In this book you will find much wisdom and comfort. Live and learn.

Best wishes

ANNE ROBINSON
Vice president of the Alzheimer's Society

Introduction

It was just before my twelfth birthday that Nan was diagnosed with Alzheimer's and came to live with us. Before that she lived in Ireland, so I didn't see her very much. My family thought that her occasional forgetfulness was just a sign of her getting older, not realizing that it was the beginning of Alzheimer's. My other grandparents died when I was very young, so unfortunately I never had the chance to get to know them. My mum used to tell us stories about Nan from her own childhood and I wished I could have spent time with her before her illness, to hear what her advice to me might have been. That's why, in autumn 2000, I started work on this book.

I decided to make a list of people who have done something inspiring with their lives. I decided to ask each person for one piece of advice, or one thought that summed up what they feel is important in life. The kind of advice that they could pass on to a grandchild – either one they have now, or maybe one that they will have in the future.

I thought that if people were kind enough to reply, I could put all their wise words into a small book and sell it to raise money to help Nan as she got worse and needed proper medical care. I also wanted to help support the researchers who are working to find a cure for Alzheimer's. If I could help, even in a small way, to prevent it from happening to someone else's nan or granddad in future, then it would all be worthwhile.

I wasn't sure how to begin and I didn't even know if anyone would write back to me! But one by one, I started writing letters to people from all walks of life. My brother Rory helped me and slowly but surely things started to happen.

The first quote we received was from Sir Stirling Moss. Then we got a phone call from Lennox Lewis's office – and that's when I started to believe that it might just work! When we received letters from Downing Street, the Vatican, the Dalai Lama and people in America and Australia, I started to realize just how many people all over the world care about the issue of Alzheimer's. It was really interesting to see what advice each person wanted to give. In one case, Tony Blair and Ian Hislop offered exactly the same advice! There are other examples of seemingly different people who actually live by the same ideals.

My plan was to be able to help Nan, as well as the Alzheimer's Society, who do such wonderful work in this field. Sadly my Nan passed away on Christmas Day 2001, but I'm sure she would be proud of me and approve of my project, which is now in her memory.

Although I don't have a piece of advice to remember her by, people who knew her before she got sick say that she was always happy. That's the way I'll remember her.

I'd like to thank Ingrid Connell at Sidgwick & Jackson for all her help, my family for their guidance and the Alzheimer's Society for supporting my project.

I'd especially like to thank everyone who was kind enough to reply to my letters, and for sharing their wisdom in this little book.

PETER VANCE
May 2003

Message to a Grandchild

PETER VANCE

I would advise my grandchild to pay attention to the following:

From quiet homes and first beginnings
Out to the undiscovered ends
There's nothing worth the wear of winning
But laughter and the love of friends...

HILAIRE BELLOC

J.K ROWLING

You are a V.S.P. = a Very Special Person,
because God loves you.
Always remember that and
behave like a V.S.P.

ARCHBISHOP DESMOND TUTU

*Always have the courage
to go with your heart.*

BOB HOSKINS

Remember that you knew them,
Not that you lost them.

SIR ARTHUR C. CLARKE

Listen.

Eric Clapton

Be your own
best friend.

JULIE WALTERS

It really is difficult to think of one piece of advice to pass on in the future but I think it would have to be the whole of *Desiderata*. It really seems to contain all the sentiments which I wish we could all adhere to.

✠ 'Go placidly amid the noise and haste, and remember what peace there may be in silence.

✠ As far as possible without surrender be on good terms with all persons.

✠ Speak your truth quietly and clearly; and listen to others, even the dull and ignorant; they too have their story.

✠ Avoid loud and aggressive persons, they are vexations to the spirit.

✠ If you compare yourself with others, you may become vain and bitter; for always there will be greater and lesser persons than yourself.

✝ Enjoy your achievements as well as your plans.

✝ Keep interested in your own career, however humble; it is a real possession in the changing fortunes of time.

✝ Exercise caution in your business affairs, for the world is full of trickery.

✝ But let this not blind you to what virtue there is; many persons strive for high ideals; and everywhere life is full of heroism.

✝ Be yourself. Especially do not feign affection.

✝ Neither be cynical about love; for in the face of all aridity and disenchantment it is as perennial as the grass.

✝ Take kindly the counsel of the years, gracefully surrendering the things of youth.

✝ Nurture strength of spirit to shield you in sudden misfortune. But do not distress yourself with imaginings.

✝ Many fears are born of fatigue and loneliness.

✝ Beyond a wholesome discipline, be gentle with
   yourself.
   You are a child of the universe,
   No less than the trees and the stars; you have a right
      to be here.
   And whether or not it is clear to you, no doubt the
      universe is unfolding as it should.

✝ Therefore be at peace with God, whatever you conceive
   Him to be, and whatever your labours and aspirations,
   in the noisy confusion of life keep peace with your soul.

✝ With all its sham, drudgery and broken dreams, it is
   still a beautiful world.

✝ Be careful. Strive to be happy.'

MAX EHRMANN, 1927

DAVID JASON

When you're young you think
nothing will change. Everyone will
always be there. This is not the case.
Always remember to spend the time
you have with your older relatives,
and not waste the time and
live to regret it.

PHIL COLLINS

If your ship doesn't come in, swim out to it.
Always remember you are unique,
  just like everyone else.
Never reach out your hand further than
  you can withdraw it.
And the best way to kill time is to work it to death.

BOB MONKHOUSE

Always
look for the
plusses.

DAME JUDI DENCH

1. Never begin to support a football team.
2. If you ever decide to write for a living, keep your decision to yourself. That way people will never know when it's not going very well.
3. Whenever possible try to make sure that you're exactly halfway through a really fantastic book.

NICK HORNBY

Always be yourself, don't try
to be someone you are not,
once you can be yourself
all the time, you will find
something very special.

BRUCE FORSYTH

*Expect anything, and should
you want things done –
do them for yourself.
Be self-sufficient and
self-supporting.*

Joan Collins

Carpe Diem -
Seize the Day.

Tony Blair

When old people tell you that things were a lot better in the old days they don't actually mean that things were a lot better in the old days; they really mean that the old days were a lot better because in the old days they were young people.

But a lot of what they say is worth listening to. With life, you don't get a second chance to go around again with the notes you made the first time, but you can use someone else's. Advice like 'never miss an opportunity to go to the lavatory' or 'sometimes it's quicker to say yes than to say no' or 'if a thing is worth doing, it's even worth doing it badly' or 'it's always worth asking' has been hard won, and is worth heeding. And so is this.

TERRY PRATCHETT

Remember that you will always be
embraced by the love of God,
and I will always love you.

GEORGE LEONARD CAREY,
former Archbishop of Canterbury

The best advice I could give a grandchild
is the advice my grandmother gave to me
when I was a lad. She always said
'be honest and true in all you do'
and I have tried to follow this advice
throughout my life.

DICKIE BIRD

Things are
changing.

Eddie Murphy

I always looked upon my granny, as my guardian angel, as any time I was in trouble at school or with my parents I would hopscotch round to Granny's for protection, as she was a star. No one ever touched me when she was there, not even my dad.

I suppose I have the same protective responsibility to my own grandchildren, it is great to hear them crying out 'Granddad' when you enter the house, I don't know how they will remember me mostly, but I am sure they will remember all the teasing I give them. It drives my wife mad when I start winding them up. It is a funny thing memory, as it can be just a simple story that has remained in the corner of your mind forever and when that particular subject comes up it pops out.

SIR ALEX FERGUSON

Energy plus talent, you're a King,
Energy but no talent, you're a Prince,
Talent, and no energy, you're a Pauper.

LORD JEFFREY ARCHER

Never look back and be sad,
but look forward to how you
can make things better.

DAME KIRI TE KANAWA

'And in the end ...
the love you save is equal
to the love you gave ...'

THE BEATLES

NORMAN COOK
(FatBoy Slim)

Life happens so fast. It begins and ends within a blink of an eye. The older we become, the more we long for yesterday and would give anything to turn the clock back. The biggest mistake we all seem to make is to become so caught up in the day to day events of life, that we forget our dreams, dreams that we cherished so much just a short time ago. Back then we felt we'd burst if they didn't come true, yet time and everyday priorities push these things aside until we dream no more. In other words we forget to be happy.

If I could leave anyone with two simple words of advice they would be simply, 'Be happy.' If I could say it in three words: 'Be happy now!!!' Take the time, make the time, once a day, every day to do something, anything that makes you and others feel more fulfilled. Work hard, sacrifice and push yourself to better yourself, but never forget how precious life is and how fast it slips away.

DAVE PELZER

Aim high!
There is little virtue in easy victory.
If you seek out challenges in life
and successfully overcome them,
it will give you much satisfaction.

Sir Edmund Hillary

My favourite piece of advice comes from *Hamlet*:
> '*This above all – to thine own self be true,*
> *And it must follow, as the night the day,*
> *Thou canst not then be false to any man.*'

What I take that to mean is: don't cheat and particularly don't cheat yourself. Always do the best you can; always be as truthful as you can; don't make excuses for yourself; be trustworthy. If you can do all that you'll probably fulfil your own potential and, what's more, you'll be able to sleep well at night and then next morning be able to look yourself in the eye in the shaving mirror.

BARRY NORMAN

Do as you would
be done by.
(I find this to be a pretty
good bit of advice.)

———————————

Sir Ranulph Fiennes

Dare to live your dreams,
try to do the harder right
rather than the easier wrong,
and always remember that
you can't help someone up a hill
without getting closer
to the top yourself.

H. NORMAN SCHWARZKOPF,
General, U.S. Army (retired)

When on
the continent,
drive on the
right-hand side
of the road.

JACK DEE

Give it your best shot
and then don't worry.

SIR JOHN HARVEY-JONES

*Take compassion as your
'keyword' through life –
and you'll stay close to goodness
all your days.*

MICHAEL CRAWFORD

Always strive for your goals
no matter how big or small.

No dream is out of your reach
if you believe in yourself.

Don't let obstacles or people
who do not believe in your
capabilities hold you back in life.

Keep your integrity, be strong
and treat others how you would
like to be treated.

LENNOX LEWIS

Be kind.

Victoria Wood

Remain honest to yourself,
but be flexible to others.

SIMON WESTON

Learn to bend with the wind
with courage and strength so that
you do not break,
but retain your sense of dignity
and learn to help others
who are not as strong as you.

VÁCLAV HAVEL,
President of the Czech Republic

Slow down.
If I could change one thing about
the way I've lived my life, I'd ease up
on the hurry sickness and make the
most of the moment. Believe me,
the future catches up with you quite
soon enough, and you don't really want
to leave yourself any room for regrets,
do you?

ANITA RODDICK

Live life as if you only have
moments left, but never treat anyone
in a way you would never want to
be treated yourself.
Be kind and thoughtful and, most
importantly, generous with your time,
and definitely never stingy with
your money, as a generous heart
leads to a whole lot of Blue Sky.

HEATHER MILLS-McCARTNEY

Have faith.
Be strong and
our dreams
can come true!

_____

Jackie Chan

*'Be honest, have courage
and be loyal to those
who deserve it.'*

MARY FRANCIS

DICK FRANCIS

You are the best in
the world at being you;
don't try to be someone else,
just try to be better at being you.
That's what being
a winner is all about.

FRANK DICK
(President of the European Athletics Coaches'
Association and author of *Winning*)

Learn the virtues of grace and kindness
and never be afraid of hard work.
To my mind there is no other
route to success.

SIR TREVOR MCDONALD

I must do the most productive thing
possible at every given moment.
This does not just mean work,
it means for a balance in
all areas of your life.

TOM HOPKINS
(author of *The Official Guide to Success*)

Never give up, because persistence pays off.
Many great ideas, inventions and projects
would never have seen the light of day
if people had given up at the first sign
of a problem or lack of response.

DAMON HILL

The advice I would give
would be in an envelope marked
'not to be opened until you are 18'.
The advice would be simple.
A few words from *Hamlet*
'to thine own self be true'.

MELVYN BRAGG

As far as my father is concerned, I think I'm going to try hard to remember him by the things that he felt were terribly important – that is, the things that interested him the most when he was still able to enjoy life. In his case, that was music, gardening, architecture and the defence of small, weak causes.

In my case, I think it's rather different. Of course I'm proud of the books in a way, but nothing like as proud as I am of my children or grandchildren. So I think that I would like to be remembered most of all in terms of relationships – family, friends and business colleagues who have almost all of them become friends. In other words, I would like to be remembered for personality rather than for achievements.

JOANNA TROLLOPE

'What we do in life,
echoes in eternity'

GLADIATOR

KRISS AKABUSI

My granddad passed on one
very good piece of advice which
I have held on to all my life.
He said, 'Never let it be said
that your mother bred a jibber.'
In other words, never give up.
I hope you never do.

ALAN TITCHMARSH

*Always
laugh
at your
mistakes.*

Darcey Bussell

Carpe diem.

IAN HISLOP

I advise people to believe in themselves,
to spiritually uplift themselves with
pleasant, positive thoughts.
Care for and love others and yourself.
Give to others and you will receive.
Have the willpower and the determination
to succeed but overall remember who
counts – you do. So have absolute faith
in your own mental, physical
and spiritual abilities.

URI GELLAR

My great aunt said to me when
I was little and had just started
drawing cartoons and making models,
'If you have a talent, no matter
how small, use it to the full.'

NICK PARK
(Aardman Animations)

Be honest
and kind.

MICHAEL WINNER

*Keep God
in the centre
of your life.*

DR STEPHEN R. COVEY

(author of *The Seven Habits
of Highly Effective People*)

The only advice I could give to any grandparent is to let your grandchild know you love them by simply hugging them, or giving them a little fuss, or tousling their hair, as I do to my eight-year-old granddaughter. Spend a little time with them telling them what it was like when you were a child, and of course if your grandchild stays with you from time to time like mine does – tell them a wonderfully silly bedtime story.

RICKY TOMLINSON

Take the time each day to have a look in your mind's eye at your dreams, aspirations and goals. Do this every day and you will find that success will come your way. Give up on this simple task and you will throw away your future.

Likewise, prior to any important event in your life, see yourself doing it well in your mind's eye. Never allow yourself to think of the opposite. Stay positive, stay focused and remember every other child deserves to dream too. Keep smiling, it only works!

JACK BLACK
(founder of MindStore)

For everyone
who has not
got a smile —
give them one
of yours.

Dale Winton

Sometimes young people feel as if nothing they can do will make a difference to the way things are. Sometimes they just don't try because they feel as if there is no hope. Peter's book shows that, if you care enough about something, you can make a huge difference in the lives of other people. We only have one lifetime to make a difference, and we owe it to ourselves and to others on this planet to try.

JOHN HOWARD,
Prime Minister of Australia

Always keep the correct perspective and balance
in your life, in all elements of your life . . .

Life is for living, loving and laughing . . .

Not whinging, whining and worrying.

Identify the things that truly matter
and raise them above all else.

Do the best you can . . . Be the best you can.

Be honest . . . Your word is the only thing
you have that is truly yours to give.

You were born outstanding . . .
so be outstanding.

STEVE MITCHELL
(founder of Partners In Business International)

My mother had Alzheimer's,
but before she did she was a very clever
businesswoman. She wasn't trained
for business in the sense that she went
to university or a smart American
business school. But I often thought her
philosophy was just as sound as anything
you could learn behind a desk.
One of her pieces of advice was, and
I quote, 'Use your head to save your legs!'
In other words if you work things
out properly before you set off
you will carry out your tasks
in the most efficient manner.

ANNE ROBINSON

My father always told me
to treat others, as I would like
to be treated in return.
I have found that, of all
the advice I have ever received,
this has been the most
practical and rewarding.

ARNOLD PALMER

Learn from the past;
live in the present;
plan for the future
(only not too much!)

Sir Alan Ayckbourn

The best advice
to myself was –
'The harder I work
the luckier I will get.'

SIR NORMAN WISDOM

Live life
to the
full!

Sir Richard Branson

*Always listen to advice
but don't always take it –
the most important person
in your life . . . is you.*

PHILIP SCHOFIELD

Each year is more important
than the next (so make it count).
Work is the failure of play
– if your work does not feel like play
you are in the wrong job.

DESMOND MORRIS

Re-examine your opinions every day
if you don't want the world to leave
you behind, but keep your belief in
sheer, unadulterated Christian kindness
as constant and inflexible as
the love you hold for your wife,
your children, your siblings, your parents
and your friends. Knowing what
should change and what should not
is the basis of a worthwhile life.

JOHN SESSIONS

'This above all – to thine own self be true,
And it must follow, as the night the day,
Thou canst not then be false to any man.'

WILLIAM SHAKESPEARE,
Hamlet, Act 1 Scene 3.

This means: always do
what you believe to be right,
not what other people say,
even if they are many.

SIR LUDOVIC KENNEDY

Do as you would be done by.
In other words, treat people as
you would like to be treated.

JUNE WHITFIELD

Never save
anything
until 'best'.
Seize each day
and live life
to the full.

LORRAINE KELLY

Remember yourself.
Know who you are and what your
purpose is for being on this earth.
Be present in each moment,
the centre of the universe.
Love yourself, be gentle
with yourself, be kind.
And,
most of all breathe deeply of life.
Just breathe.

MICHAEL E. GERBER
(author of *The E-Myth: Why Most Small Businesses
Don't Work and What to Do About It*)

Never, ever, give up!

Pete Postlethwaite

If I could give one thing to a grandchild to remember me by when I'm gone – here's what it would be. Remember that love from one heart to another is the most beautiful way of living. And if you connect and never separate yourself from faith in God, you will live a truly happy life. And if there's a time when you cannot find God or feel God, look for someone who needs a helping hand, or a word of encouragement. Give yourself to this lonely or hurting soul and you will be living out the love of God and then you will feel a wonderful and beautiful feeling go through your whole personality. That feeling will be the presence of God blessing you for what you are doing.

Dr Robert H. Schuller

(author of *Tough Times Never Last, But Tough People Do!*)

Of all the human virtues,
the greatest is courage.
Without courage all other virtues –
compassion, generosity, loyalty –
will retreat into helplessness
if confronted by a threat.
Therefore hold to your courage
in standing up for those things
you know to be right, and always
remember that there is nothing
to fear but fear itself.

FREDERICK FORSYTH

Never take the path
of least resistance.
Live your life for now
and not the future
and learn to love yourself
as well as those
close to you.

WILL CARLING

The truth be told, if you asked me every day for a week, and I could forget my answers, I might give a different one every day. If it were my grandchild, I would spend our relationship trying to open their eyes to an infinite number of pieces of advice.

1. Never measure your wealth in terms of money and power – true wealth is a by-product of your sweet friendships, your romance with nature and your marriage to the arts.
2. Make it all fun!
3. Feel the privileges of life and grow with gratitude.
4. Get good and tender with kissing.
5. Create and follow your dreams no matter what.
6. Live in service to humankind and nature.
7. Never whine or be cynical.

DR HUNTER (PATCH) ADAMS MD
(founder of The Gesundheit Institute, USA)

Always make a difference.
Don't be afraid to show your feelings.
Respect your fellow human being.

AINSLEY HARRIOTT

The only piece of advice I am ever tempted to offer in life is 'beware of those who give advice' . . . but Raymond's gran (in *The Wrong Boy*) is full of wise words and advice:

'So my Gran told us about Giuseppe Garibaldi and how he had to cross the Straits of Messina before Italy could become united. But all that Garibaldi had was a leaking ship, a few ragged volunteers, hardly any weapons and nowt but a couple of salami sandwiches between the lot of them.

   "And that's why", my Gran said, "nobody ever thought he'd ever do it. Nobody believed he'd ever amount to much. But you see, lads, what nobody ever saw, not until it was too late, was that

Giuseppe Garibaldi and his volunteers, inside of them they had something that more than made up for the lack of salami or the want of proper weapons; they had unity, they had purpose; and they had love for each other."

My Gran nodded at us. She said, "And you lads, always try and remember that. Remember that you've got love for each other. And if you can keep hold of that, boys, if you can go on looking after each other, you'll always find a way to cross the Straits of Messina.'"

WILLY RUSSELL

Be honest.

Sir Stirling Moss

Treat others as
you would like
to be treated.

SALLY GUNNELL

*Your dreams are
the blueprint
of reality.*

GREG NORMAN

If you want to do something,
ask yourself two questions.

1. Is your proposed action sensible?
2. Will it hurt or inconvenience anybody?

If the answers are
(1.) Yes and (2.) No, do it.
If not, don't!

SIR PATRICK MOORE

It is better to regret
something you did
rather than something
you didn't do!
Nothing ventured –
nothing gained.

SIR TERENCE CONRAN

If there is something you really
love doing – it might be painting,
it might be playing a musical instrument;
in my case it was climbing –
follow that passion to the full.
Work to become good at it and
most important of all, enjoy it.

SIR CHRISTIAN BONINGTON

If someone does you
99% wrong and 1% good,
you should always
remember the good.

LINFORD CHRISTIE

You make your own progress
and your own luck. By determination,
commitment, refusal to give up or
be straightjacketed by convention
or the short-sightedness of others —
describe it as you will — you are the one
who creates the airflow beneath
your own wings.

RICHARD NOBLE
(supersonic world land-speed record holder)

Be curious – there is always more to know,

Be interested – there is always more to learn,

Be active and engaged – and your life
will be fuller for it.

RORY BREMNER

You are unencumbered
by the preconceptions that
age and experience bring.

So use that freedom
to make a difference.

Be creative and be courageous, and
don't be afraid to take risks: mistakes
should be learnt from – not feared.

JAMES DYSON

God's Presence
surrounds you
every day.

RUTH STAFFORD PEALE
(co-founder of Guideposts, USA,
wife of the late Dr Norman Vincent Peale,
author of *The Power of Positive Thinking*)

When dealing with others,
use your heart.
When dealing with yourself,
use your head.

———————————

Bryan Adams

Treat other people
in the way you'd like to
be treated yourself.

PAM AYRES

Every day of your life is to be
approached with enthusiasm and willing.
Do so, and everyone will be lifted and
enlightened. Don't let the attitudes
of others affect your own determination
to enjoy life, but always remember to
consider the feelings of those around you.

DAVID GOWER

I do remember one bit of advice
that I was given by my Granddad
many, many years ago which was,
'You're only here once, it's not a rehearsal,
so make every second count . . .
and don't forget to stop
and smell the flowers!'

CHRIS TARRANT

We live but once (not everyone agrees with that) and I think it is terrible to waste that single opportunity – so it's important not to give ourselves cause for regret. I hate to hear people say, 'I always wanted to . . . but . . .', and you can fill in the dots for yourself – I always wanted to sail the Atlantic? Write a book? Dance on a beach under the moonlight? Learn to fly? Eat jellied eels? You want do something? If it hurts no one, do it.

BERNARD CORNWELL

Love and stay true to your friends
and family. Always be prepared to
put your money where your mouth
is. The advice my father gave to me
and his father gave to him: everyday
when you become a man you will
have to shave. You will have to look
yourself in the face in the mirror.
And if you can do that with a clear
conscience, to hell with what the
rest of the world thinks of you.

RICHARD LITTLEJOHN

Although my grandparents lived quite a long way from my home I always took the opportunity to visit them regularly. I never regret asking my grandmother about her life and I discovered many interesting things.

I would recommend to any grandchild that they should take any opportunity to question their grandparents about their lives, because once they have gone that opportunity will be lost forever. You never know what you might discover.

TERRY WAITE

Everything changes.
The only thing that doesn't
change is the fact that
everything changes.

JONATHAN ROSS

Good, Better, Best
Never ever rest
Till your good is better
And your better is best.

———————————————————

Gary Lineker

What goes around,
comes around.

JULIAN RICHER
(Chairman, Richer Sounds International)

Remember that your
mum and dad are always
your best friends.

SIR HENRY COOPER

I have always done my best to view problems
as challenges and to never lose hope.
I've always believed that a good challenge
presents new opportunities – opportunities
to learn, to grow, to gain strength,
or to reach a higher goal.
And I've always believed that
the future is in God's hands.

RICHARD M. DeVOS
(co-founder, Amway Corporation)

Education is paramount in today's society.
It is essential that the opportunity of
learning is grasped with both hands.
Life will deliver back a percentage
of the input effort, the more you put in
the more you receive in return.

STEPHEN HENDRY

*Sport and life are to
be enjoyed to the full.
Sport is better
than working!*

———————————————

Ian Botham

To a young person, a week
can seem like a year.
To an older person, a year
seems to pass in a few days.
Enjoy and use your life
while the days are long.

MICHAEL ASPEL

Always treat others
the way you would like
them to treat you.

MURRAY WALKER

No one in the world
is exactly like you are –
you're unique and that
makes you special –
be yourself.

DAVID ESSEX

Enjoy life, don't worry,
because more than half the
things people worry about
never happen.

DES O'CONNOR

Learn the four R's:

1. Reading
2. Riting (!)
3. Reckoning Up (without a calculator)
4. Right and wrong (and the difference between)

SIR JIMMY SAVILE

My grandmother has always
taught me to be proud of who
I am and where I come from, and
through her my mother has always
encouraged me to believe in myself.
See good in others, even when it is
hard, but most of all, 'Walk a mile
in someone else's shoes.'
Wise words.

MARTINE McCUTCHEON

Live each day
as if it's your last,
as one day it will be.

Jonah Lomu

It is so important that we instil in our children and grandchildren the value of friendship. Like young trees, our hopes for the future are to see the saplings of friendship take root and flourish, so that new friendships endure and prosper. And though we may be separated by a great distance as we get older, those bonds of friendship will remain with us for the rest of our lives.

MARY McALEESE,
President of Ireland

I would say without a doubt,
to read Eckhart Tolle's *The Power of Now*
and learn how to live in the moment.
There is no other way to transcend
the human plane of suffering
than by living in the Now.

GILLIAN ANDERSON

Always think of others, not just yourself.

Alan Shearer

Mistakes are only
bad if you don't
learn from them.

DAVINA McCALL

Life is a challenge, every day offers new reasons to quit or stop trying. However, it is important to remember that the easiest thing in the world is to come up with an excuse not to do something. I found that the most important thing in life is to stop saying, 'I wish' and start saying, 'I will'.

Whenever I pursue my dreams, I discover something astonishing – I discover myself. My secret is to consider nothing impossible, and to treat possibilities as probabilities. There are two ways I can live my life: following my dreams or doing something else. I choose to follow my dreams. Remember passion is everything. Take your passion, combine it with your gifts, and you will be explosive, unstoppable, an inspiration.

DAVID COPPERFIELD

*Grandchildren, make sure
you ask your grandparents
to describe as much as they
can about their childhoods.*

STEPHEN FRY

You may read about the
'rich and famous' and be inspired
to achieve that kind of success
for yourself. And you should chase
that vision. But always remember
two things: firstly, that it's far more
important to be loved than to be rich
or famous; and, secondly, to receive
love you must first give it.

SIR CLIFF RICHARD

Find joy in showing concern
for other people and in
living according to God's law.

POPE JOHN PAUL II

My grandmother always said, 'You get out of life what you put into it.' To me this means that whatever you choose to do, you should always work as hard as you can at it and give the best that you can give. I have always tried to do this in all that I do. This way I may be disappointed if I don't get what I want, but I know that I have tried my best and need to try harder!

PAULA RADCLIFFE

Never give up
No matter what is going on
Never give up
Develop the heart
Too much energy in your country
Is spent developing the mind
Instead of the heart
Develop the heart
Be compassionate
Not just to your friends
But to everyone
Be compassionate
Work for peace
In your heart
And in the world
Work for peace
And I say again
Never give up
No matter what is going on around you
Never give up.

H.H. THE XIVTH DALAI LAMA

I've learnt to have a sense of faith in the fact that people really do care – even really famous people who, though extremely busy, have still taken the time to help someone like me, whom they don't even know.

I've also learned the value of setting a goal, even if it looks unlikely that I'll be able to achieve it. And I've learned not to lose heart when it seems that things are going badly, or when people say no.

Most of all, I've learned that if I want to succeed, I shouldn't be afraid to keep on trying. Many of the people who wrote back, including world champions, talked about the value of persistence and never giving up. That's something I'll always try to remember.

PETER VANCE

My mum told me that the one piece
of advice Nan gave to her children was;
'If you do nothing else, make sure
you say one prayer every day.
Every prayer is heard.'

CHRISTINA MONAGHAN
(Peter's Nan)

The Alzheimer's Society

Peter's project aims to help in the fight against Alzheimer's disease. Peter Vance, from Bristol, England, devised the project when he was just fourteen years old to raise money to care for his nan and to support the Alzheimer's Society.

The Alzheimer's Society is the leading national care and research charity for people with all forms of dementia, their families and carers.

The Society was started in 1979 by a group of carers and professionals. It is an organization with over 25,000 members which is governed by trustees elected by the membership. There are 300 local branches and support groups carrying out the work of the Alzheimer's Society throughout England, Wales and Northern Ireland.

One in four people know or have known someone with Alzheimer's disease or dementia. This means there are over thirteen million people in the UK whose partners, parents, grandparents, friends and loved ones are directly affected by a set of diseases which are, as yet, incurable.

The Alzheimer's Society has unique knowledge and understanding of the impact dementia has on those with the disease, their families and carers. We provide support, information services and quality home and day care. We also campaign, raise awareness and fund research into cause, cure and care.

The Alzheimer's Society runs a national helpline, which provides information, advice, support and referrals to anyone with concerns about Alzheimer's disease or any other form of dementia. It is open from 8.30 a.m to 6.30 p.m on weekdays.

We depend on donations to ensure that the very special services provided by the Society continue to be there for those who need them most.

How to contact the Alzheimer's Society

Alzheimer's Society website www.alzheimers.org.uk

Alzheimer's Society Helpline 0845 300 0336

Alzheimer's Society membership enquiries 0845 306 0868

Alzheimer's Society donation hotline 0845 306 0898

You can write to us at
Alzheimer's Society
Gordon House
10 Greencoat Place
London SW1P 1PH
United Kingdom

All other enquiries
Main telephone number 020 7306 0606
Fax 020 7306 0808
Email enquiries@alzheimers.org.uk

Alzheimer's Society
Registered Charity No. 296645. A company limited by
guarantee and registered in England, number 2115499.